CLASS 58 LOCOMOTIVES

Andrew Cole

AMBERLEY

No. 58002, 4 August 1999
No. 58002 passes Washwood Heath light engine carrying Mainline blue livery. This loco carries stickers for the Worksop Aberdonian Railtour, which ran on 21 September 1996.

First published 2016

Amberley Publishing
The Hill, Stroud
Gloucestershire, GL5 4EP

www.amberley-books.com

Copyright © Andrew Cole, 2016

The right of Andrew Cole to be identified as the Author of this work has been asserted in accordance with the Copyrights, Designs and Patents Act 1988.

ISBN 978 1 4456 6212 1 (print)
ISBN 978 1 4456 6213 8 (ebook)

British Library Cataloguing in Publication Data.
A catalogue record for this book is available from the British Library.

Typesetting by Amberley Publishing.
Printed in the UK.

Introduction

The Class 58 story dates back to the late 1970s, when British Rail wanted a new class of loco that was cheap to build and also easy to maintain. British Rail also saw the loco as a potential export design but, unfortunately, no orders were forthcoming. The Class 58 build was awarded to British Rail Engineering Limited at their Doncaster Works. As a result, the last twenty Class 56 locomotives had to be built at Crewe instead of Doncaster.

Fifty locomotives were to be built to a modular design, a concept that was new to British Rail, wherein the different components could be replaced easily. They were built to a Co-Co wheel design, and were all fitted with Ruston Paxman 12RK3ACT engines, which they carried throughout their lives. The first loco was delivered in 1983, with the rest of the class being delivered by 1987.

The last loco, No. 58050, was experimentally fitted with SEPEX wheelslip equipment, although this was removed before it entered service. The equipment was later fitted to the Class 60s. No. 58050 was to be the last locomotive to be built at the famous Doncaster Works.

All fifty locomotives were delivered in red-stripe Railfreight livery, and all would later be repainted into Trainload coal livery. Upon sectorisation, all would pass to the Mainline Freight division. A handful of locomotives received the attractive aircraft blue Mainline livery, but most just had Mainline branding applied to the Trainload coal livery.

EWS would later take control of the three British freight companies, bringing them all under one roof, and in doing so inherited all fifty Class 58s. Again, a small handful would be repainted into EWS maroon livery, starting with No. 58050, which was painted for the Toton open day in 1998. Despite the class proving themselves to be very reliable, it was decided to place members into storage from 1999 onwards and, by 2002, all members of the class had been taken out of use and stored, with the last member stored in September 2002.

Despite the future looking bleak, a requirement was soon identified for heavy freight locomotives for use in Continental Europe on ballast trains, in connection with the construction of high-speed lines. Nine would be sent to work in Spain for operator GIF. They would later be sold to Transfesa, while another three are currently in store at Albacete, Spain, with little prospect of them ever returning to the UK.

Meanwhile, another twenty-four locomotives would find use with Axiom Rail in France, although all of these are now in storage at Alizay in northern France, with one in storage at Woippy yard, also in France. Again, there is little hope of these locomotives returning to the UK. The stored locomotives in France include three that were sent to the Netherlands to work for ACTS; when the contract had finished, they moved to France.

At least one member of the class has been preserved, with No. 58016 being owned by the Class 58 loco group. They also purchased No. 58045 for spares before sending the remains for scrap. DB Schenker finally sold its remaining five UK-based Class 58s, with three being sold for scrap, and the remaining two sold privately.

What follows is a pictorial tribute to a modern workhorse that finished work far too early.

No. 58001, 3 December 1984

No. 58001 rests at Saltley depot, Birmingham, carrying red-stripe Railfreight livery. This loco was released from works in February 1983 and, like all other members of the class, was released in this livery. It would later gain Trainload Coal livery, and is currently stored at Alizay in northern France.

No. 58001, 9 October 1988

No. 58001 is seen on display at Bescot open day, 1988. The loco has now been repainted into Trainload Coal livery, a livery that all members of the class would receive after the red-stripe Railfreight livery.

No. 58001, 29 August 1989

No. 58001 approaches Nuneaton, carrying Trainload Coal livery, with an MGR working from the north. The Class 58s were synonymous with coal working throughout their BR careers, although, later on, they would find employment on many different types of traffic.

Nos 58001 and 82126, 28 June 1990

No. 58001 passes Washwood Heath while employed on a West Coast drag from Birmingham New Street to Nuneaton. These workings were common when the OHLE was under repair between Birmingham and Rugby, and Class 58s were often the motive power used.

No. 58001, 10 July 1994

No. 58001 is seen under repair inside Doncaster Works. Doncaster undertook all repairs to the class during BR days. The loco has had its Ruston Paxman 12RK3ACT engine removed for repair in another area of the works.

No. 58001, 15 November 2008

No. 58001 stands at Barrow Hill, having been repainted back into its original red-stripe Railfreight livery. This loco would be sent to work in France on high-speed-line construction work, and is currently stored at Alizay in northern France, carrying ETF (Eurovia Travaux Ferroviaries) livery.

No. 58002, 15 May 1983

No. 58002 is seen when brand new at Doncaster Works. At this time the loco had only done a few test runs, and was waiting release to Toton for crew training. This was the first day I saw a Class 58, and was bowled over by the bright new livery.

No. 58002, 15 May 1983

No. 58002 stands in the yard at Doncaster Works when brand new. At the time the livery really stood out, as it was one of the first changes from standard BR blue livery.

No. 58002, 6 July 1984

No. 58002 rests at Saltley depot, Birmingham, carrying red-stripe Railfreight livery. Saltley was to become familiar with the class, due to the large amount of MGR coal traffic in the area.

No. 58002, 17 March 1988

No. 58002 is seen at Lawley Street container terminal, Birmingham, on the day it was named *Daw Mill Colliery*. The loco had been repainted into Trainload Coal livery, and it is interesting to note that it had received a set of bogies from a later member of the class, the tell-tale sign being the visible sand boxes. When new, these bogies were only fitted to No. 58036 onwards.

No. 58002, 30 June 1988

No. 58002 is seen stabled outside the office block at Saltley depot, Birmingham. The loco carries the name *Daw Mill Colliery*; also of note is the Toton depot plaque in the middle of the loco.

No. 58002, 2 April 2009

No. 58002 is seen in the scrap line at Eastleigh depot, contemplating its future. By this time the loco had been repainted into Mainline blue livery, and would spend thirteen years in storage before finally being cut up at Eastleigh by European Metal Recycling in December 2013. It is one of nine Class 58s to have been scrapped.

No. 58003, 20 June 1984

No. 58003 is seen at Lawley Street container terminal, Birmingham. The class was ordered mainly for coal traffic but, unfortunately, the first members of the class were delivered during the miners' strike. Consequently, they could be found on other traffic until MGR workings resumed.

No. 58003, 12 January 1985

No. 58003 rests at Bescot, carrying red-stripe Railfreight livery, with snow still on the ground. This loco would later go on to be named *Markham Colliery*.

No. 58003, 28 July 1992

No. 58003 is seen approaching the yard at Washwood Heath with a short rake of two-axle diesel oil tanks. This was a local trip working from the nearby Saltley depot, producing any type of loco that was spare on the depot. The loco carries Trainload Coal livery and also the name *Markham Colliery*. This is another Class 58 that was scrapped, this time in August 2010 by European Metal Recycling at Kingsbury.

No. 58004, 15 May 1983

No. 58004 is seen under construction at Doncaster Works. The class was built to a modular design, meaning that components could be removed and replaced easily. It would be another three months before No. 58004 was ready to leave the works.

No. 58004, 17 August 1984

No. 58004 is seen stabled at Saltley, carrying red-stripe Railfreight livery. Of note is No. 25037 behind, of a class that the 58s helped to eliminate.

No. 58004, 25 August 1989

No. 58004 is seen five years after the previous photograph, again at Saltley depot; by this time, however, it had been repainted into Trainload Coal livery. When freshly applied, this livery suited the class really well.

No. 58004, 8 February 2014

No. 58004 is seen in long-term storage at Alizay, northern France. There are currently twenty-three members of the class stored at this depot, with little hope of returning to the UK. They were hired to Axiom Rail, who painted them into various different liveries, with No. 58004 carrying TSO (Travaux du Sud-Ouest) livery.

No. 58005, 2 February 1985

No. 58005 is seen resting at Bescot, carrying red-stripe Railfreight livery, sandwiched between two BR blue Class 56 locos. Later in life, this loco received the name *Ironbridge Power Station*, and would spend many years in storage at Leicester before being reactivated and sent to work in France for Axiom Rail. It is currently in storage at Alizay, northern France, carrying ETF livery.

No. 58006, 1 August 1984

No. 58006 is seen in the summer sunshine at Saltley depot, Birmingham, while on crew training duty. At the time, Saltley used to be a major depot in the Midlands, but now has been reduced to a short spur. All the depot buildings have been demolished, leaving just a couple of portacabins as a train-crew booking-on point.

Nos 58006 and 58003, 3 August 1992

No. 58006 is seen approaching Washwood Heath yard while double-heading an MGR working along with classmate No. 58003 *Markham Colliery*. Despite having the multiple working cables on the front, the class were never regular double headers, being capable of hauling most trains singularly.

No. 58006, 30 August 1998

No. 58006 is seen at rest at Saltley depot. The loco carries former Trainload Coal livery, but the decals have been replaced with Mainline branding. Only a few members of the class would receive the full Mainline blue livery. Of note are the replacement bogies that have been fitted, which have come from a later member of the class, these being fitted new to No. 58036 onwards only.

No. 58006, 20 August 1999

No. 58006 is seen passing through one of the through roads at Doncaster with a rake of two-axle sand-carrying wagons. This loco would only have another four months of service left, being stored in December 1999. It would be another member of the class to be sent to France, on hire to Axiom Rail; it is currently stored at Alizay depot, carrying ETF livery.

No. 58006, 8 February 2014

No. 58006 is seen carrying ETF livery at Alizay depot, northern France, while in long-term storage. The loco is on hire to Axiom Rail for high-speed-line construction work but, like all twenty-three members of the class in storage, there is not much hope of them returning to use. Of note is that, by now, the later bogies that were fitted have been replaced with an earlier set.

No. 58007, 10 September 1984

No. 58007 is seen stabled at Saltley depot, carrying red-stripe Railfreight livery. The class were regular visitors to Saltley, due to the MGR traffic in the area, consisting mainly of Daw Mill Colliery and Didcot Power Station workings.

No. 58007, 8 July 1990

No. 58007 is seen at Saltley depot, having not long been repainted into Trainload Coal livery. The following month this loco would receive the name *Drakelow Power Station*. This is another member of the class currently stored at Alizay, northern France, where it carries TSO livery.

No. 58008, 11 September 1984

No. 58008 is seen stabled at Saltley, carrying red-stripe Railfreight livery. This loco had only been in use for about nine months, and still looks very respectable. Resident No. 25027, which has been long withdrawn, can be seen behind.

No. 58008, 12 September 1984

No. 58008 rests at Saltley, carrying red-stripe Railfreight livery. As can be seen, this livery certainly stood out at the time compared to the standard BR blue-liveried locos in the background. At this time, Saltley was a major depot for both passenger and freight workings in the West Midlands, and I am now privileged to work with staff from Saltley who worked during this time.

No. 58008, 12 February 1990

No. 58008 is seen passing Washwood Heath with an MGR working. This view shows the loco in typical work-stained appearance, hard at work doing what it was built for. Today there are no Class 58s in use in the UK, and all the MGR wagons have been withdrawn and mostly scrapped.

No. 58008, 3 August 1992

No. 58008 is seen restarting its loaded MGR working at Washwood Heath, following a signal check. By this time, the loco had received Trainload Coal livery; this working was probably heading for Didcot Power Station.

No. 58008, 15 September 1996

No. 58008 is seen stabled at Hither Green depot, London. This loco carries Mainline blue livery, one of just a handful of Class 58s to do so. All fifty locos passed to Mainline from British Rail.

No. 58008, 12 April 1999

No. 58008 is seen stabled at Saltley depot, carrying Mainline blue livery. This livery really suited the class, but only a handful of locos received it. At the time of writing, No. 58008 is at Eastleigh being stripped for spare parts, and will become the ninth member of the class to be scrapped.

No. 58009, 5 May 1984

No. 58009 is seen stabled at Saltley depot, carrying red-stripe Railfreight livery. This loco had only been in service for three months.

No. 58009, 24 May 1984

No. 58009 departs Lawley Street container terminal, having just arrived with a loaded working. The class were used on various workings early on in their careers due to there not being any coal traffic as a result of the miners' strike.

No. 58009, 17 November 1988

No. 58009 rests at Saltley depot, carrying Trainload Coal livery. This loco had just been released from works overhaul, and still looks immaculate.

No. 58009, 27 October 1999

No. 58009 is seen passing Washwood Heath with a rake of loaded cartic wagons from the Rover Works at Longbridge. By this time, the loco had had its Trainload Coal logos replaced with Mainline logos. Today the Class 58s are no more; the Rover car plant has closed and even the gasholders behind the loco have been demolished.

No. 58009, 8 February 2014

No. 58009 is seen in long-term storage at Alizay, northern France, carrying TSO livery. This loco, and the other twenty-two present, haven't turned a wheel for many years, and would probably need a lot spending on them if they were ever to return to service.

No. 58010, 5 October 1984

No. 58010 is seen stabled at Saltley, carrying red-stripe Railfreight livery. Despite only being in traffic for less than twelve months, the red stripe has already started peeling off.

No. 58010, 29 August 1990

No. 58010 rests at Saltley, carrying Trainload Coal livery. Of note is that the eight in the running number has been changed to a three! This loco is currently in storage at Alizay, northern France, carrying TSO livery.

No. 58011, 8 May 1984

No. 58011 is seen at Saltley depot, Birmingham, carrying red-stripe Railfreight livery. Behind can be seen a Class 45, another class that the 58s helped to eliminate.

No. 58011, 17 May 1984

No. 58011 passes Saltley depot with a rake of domestic coal hoppers. The class were never common on this type of coal hopper, being more at home on the MGR type of hoppers.

No. 58011, 22 October 1984

No. 58011 is seen passing Saltley depot, this time at the head of a rake of two-axle diesel tank wagons. This view shows the different variety of work that the class had early in their careers. No. 58011 would later go on to be named *Worksop Depot*.

No. 58011, 7 February 1986

No. 58011 rests at a cold-looking Saltley depot after a light fall of snow. After being in service for two years, the loco is now starting to look a bit weather worn.

No. 58011, 26 January 1989

No. 58011 is seen stabled at Saltley depot, having not long been through works for overhaul and repaint into Trainload Coal livery. This loco would later be named *Worksop Depot*, and is yet another member of the class to be found stored at Alizay in northern France. The loco currently carries TSO livery.

No. 58012, 13 June 1984

No. 58012 is seen stabled at Saltley, alongside No. 25224. The Class 58 had only been in traffic for three months, and the Class 25 had only two years left in service.

No. 58012, 13 June 1984

No. 58012 is seen later on the same day from the previous photograph, and is seen departing Lawley Street container terminal with a loaded working. After the MGR traffic picked up again, the use of Class 58s on container trains dropped off.

No. 58012, 9 July 1984

No. 58012 is seen at Saltley depot, in company with a BR blue Class 31. The livery certainly stood out on a gloomy day, and the large cab-side numbers were a great help from a distance.

No. 58012, 19 January 1985

No. 58012 is seen stabled in the snow at Bescot. The class could be found in large numbers at Bescot, especially at the weekends when coal traffic was slow. No. 58012 would be stored in 1999, and has recently been sold by DB Cargo, firstly to Ron Hull Junior Rotherham for scrap. However, it has since moved, along with classmate No. 58023, to the Battlefield Line, Shackerstone.

No. 58013, 4 June 1984

No. 58013 is seen at Saltley depot while on crew-training duty. This loco would suffer derailment damage in 1987, which kept it out of traffic for twelve months before being repaired, during which time it was used as a source of spare parts for other members of the class, before being returned to service.

No. 58013, 13 April 1985

No. 58013 is seen at its home depot of Toton, along with other members of the class. Toton was always home to the class, with none being allocated elsewhere until Eastleigh gained a few of the class very late on in their careers. No. 58013 is currently stored at Alizay, northern France, carrying ETF livery.

No. 58013, 5 March 1991

No. 58013 is seen passing Washwood Heath light engine, heading for the nearby Saltley depot. This was one of the last members of the class to carry the original red-stripe Railfreight livery and, as can be seen, it has had a replacement engine-room door fitted that carries Trainload Coal livery.

No. 58014, 28 June 1984

No. 58014 is seen departing Landore Street container terminal with a loaded container working. This loco was less than three months old at the time, and had spent the first two months in use as a crew-training loco at Reading.

No. 58014, 19 January 1985

No. 58014 is seen stabled in the snow at Bescot during the winter of 1985. No. 58014 would later go on to be named *Didcot Power Station*.

No. 58014, 7 August 1988

No. 58014 is seen stabled at Bescot at the head of a line of six class members. By this time, the loco had been repainted into Trainload Coal livery, and carries the name *Didcot Power Station*. All the other five locos in the line still carry red-stripe Railfreight livery.

No. 58014, 22 September 1988

No. 58014 is seen in Trainload Coal livery at Saltley, having been refueled; it is now heading for the stabling roads. This loco is one of the nine members of the class that have been scrapped, this one being cut up by European Metal Recycling, Kingsbury, in August 2010.

No. 58015, 28 July 1984

No. 58015 is seen on display at Doncaster Works open day 1984. This loco was brand new at the time, and had yet to be released to traffic; it wouldn't be for another couple of weeks.

No. 58015, 1 November 1984

No. 58015 departs Lawley Street container terminal with a loaded container working. These sidings are still in use today with Freightliner for container traffic.

No. 58015, 2 February 1991

No. 58015 passes Washwood Heath with a loaded MGR working heading for Didcot Power Station. By this time, the loco has received Trainload Coal livery. At the time, these workings were an everyday occurrence; it's hard to believe that today the number of coal workings on the network is shrinking.

No. 58015, 29 December 1991

No. 58015 is seen stabled at Saltley depot, carrying Trainload Coal livery. Today this loco is one of eight members of the class that have been sold to Transfesa, currently working on Spanish high-speed construction trains, based in Alicante, Spain. It carries the number L54.

No. 58016, 16 February 1985

No. 58016 rests in the snow at Bescot, carrying red-stripe Railfreight livery. At the time, this loco had been in service for less than six months.

No. 58016, 4 May 1985

No. 58016 is seen passing Saltley depot at the head of a rake of empty Freightliner wagons. At this time the class could be found working many different types of trains, from container workings to oil trains.

No. 58016, 8 May 1985

No. 58016 is seen just four days after the previous photograph, this time approaching Saltley with a loaded MGR working, bound for Didcot Power Station. This loco would eventually be sent to work in France, along with various other members of the class, working for Fertis.

No. 58016, 3 May 1997

No. 58016 is seen at Knottingley depot, having been repainted into EW&S maroon livery. Only a small handful of Class 58s carried this livery, and eventually the '&' was dropped, with later members carrying EWS signage.

No. 58016, 22 March 1999

No. 58016 is seen stabled outside the office building at Saltley, carrying EW&S maroon livery. EWS took over the majority of the UK freight operations in 1996.

No. 58016, 17 November 2012

No. 58016 is seen inside the roundhouse at Barrow Hill, carrying Fertis livery. When this loco returned from use in France, it was successfully preserved and, to date, is the only member of the class to be preserved. It moved to Barrow Hill, a place it would have visited many times in its BR career, for initial restoration, but it has since moved to Leicester.

No. 58016, 16 March 2016

No. 58016 is seen stabled at Leicester depot. This Class 58 is the sole member of the class to have been preserved, and has moved to the UK Rail depot at Leicester for restoration. No. 58016 is owned by the Class 58 Locomotive Group, and is a welcome addition to the list of UK preserved locos.

No. 58017, 15 December 1984

No. 58017 is seen when only two months old at Saltley depot, Birmingham, and is still looking very clean. Most members of the class visited Saltley, due to the amount of coal traffic in the Midlands with power stations at Didcot, Rugeley and Ironbridge.

No. 58017, 2 February 1985
No. 58017 is seen stabled for the weekend at Bescot, carrying red-stripe Railfreight livery. No. 58017 has become one of the class that has been scrapped, this being completed by European Metal Recycling at Eastleigh depot in January 2014.

No. 58017, 22 January 1988
No. 58017 is seen in the snow at Saltley depot, along with classmate No. 58024. No. 58017 would later go on to be named *Eastleigh Depot*.

No. 58017, 7 December 1989

No. 58017 is seen ticking over outside the office block at Saltley depot, having just been released from works overhaul, which included a repaint into Trainload Coal livery. When clean, this was another livery, which suited the class.

No. 58017, 17 May 1991

No. 58017 approaches Olton station, near Solihull, on the main line between Birmingham and Leamington Spa, with an empty MGR working from Didcot power station. This was the main traffic for which the class was built, and they did the job successfully for many years until the arrival of the Class 66s.

No. 58017, 30 August 1998

No. 58017 rests at Saltley depot, wearing the name *Eastleigh Depot*. The loco carries Trainload Coal livery, but has had the logos replaced with Mainline logos. This loco would be scrapped in January 2014 at Eastleigh by European Metal Recycling.

No. 58018, 23 October 1998

No. 58018 is seen passing through Doncaster with a loaded MGR working. No. 58018 carries the name *High Marnham Power Station*, and also carries Trainload Coal livery, but with the logos replaced by Mainline logos. Doncaster was always a good hunting ground for the class, due to the high volume of coal workings through the station. No. 58018 is currently stored at Alizay, northern France, carrying TSO livery.

No. 58019, 28 July 1984

No. 58019 is seen at Doncaster Works while still under construction. It would be another five months before the loco was ready to enter service.

No. 58019, 9 April 1985

No. 58019 is seen waiting to depart from Lawley Street container terminal with a loaded container working. This would later gain the name *Shirebrook Colliery*.

No. 58019, 1 February 1991

No. 58019 rests outside Saltley depot, having been named *Shirebrook Colliery* just over twelve months previously. This loco would be scrapped by European Metal Recycling at their Kingsbury site in October 2010.

No. 58020, 13 April 1985

No. 58020 is seen stabled at its home depot of Toton, along with various other classmates. The loco carries *Doncaster Works BRE* nameplates, which would later be changed to just *Doncaster Works*. Of note are the second-series bogies fitted to No. 58020, the only one with them fitted from new before No. 58036.

No. 58020, 30 June 1985

No. 58020 is seen stabled at Saltley, carrying the name *Doncaster Works BRE*. This view also shows the higher positioning of the 'Railfreight' logo to accommodate the nameplate. No. 58020 would eventually be sold to Transfesa, and can currently be found working in Spain.

No. 58020, 10 September 1986

No. 58020 is seen at Saltley, having had its original *Doncaster Works BRE* nameplate replaced with a *Doncaster Works* plate. This view is dated September 1986, but most publications have the name change down as from May 1987. This shot also shows the loco had yet to be fitted with a cast Railfreight logo on the cab front.

No. 58020, 5 April 1987

No. 58020 *Doncaster Works* is seen stabled outside the office block at Saltley depot. By this time, along with the name change, the loco has now been fitted with a cast Railfreight logo on the cab front.

No. 58020, 15 July 1988

No. 58020 departs Lawley Street container terminal with a loaded container working. The loco carries the name *Doncaster Works*, and still carries the later type of bogie with the sandboxes on the outside.

No. 58020, 12 July 1992

No. 58020 is seen inside Doncaster Works during the open day of 1992. The loco's Ruston Paxman 12RK3ACT engine has been removed for repair elsewhere inside the works. The loco also carries the name *Doncaster Works*. Doncaster always undertook heavy repairs to the Class 58s.

No. 58021, 1 February 1985

No. 58021 is seen stabled at Saltley, carrying red-stripe Railfreight livery. This view shows clearly the large amount of bodyside doors fitted to the class to gain access for maintenance purposes.

No. 58021, 16 February 1985

No. 58021 stands in the snow at Saltley depot, along with various other classes of loco. Today this view has completely changed, with all the track lifted and the shed buildings demolished. Hard to imagine that, in steam days, this depot had three roundhouses.

No. 58021, 19 July 1985

No. 58021 is seen at Lawley Street container terminal, shunting its rake of empty flat wagons ready for loading. No. 58021 would later be named *Hither Green Depot*.

No. 58021, 30 July 1992

A work-stained No. 58021 is seen moving off from a signal check at Washwood Heath with a loaded MGR working for Didcot power station. The loco carries Trainload Coal livery.

No. 58021, 26 June 1993

No. 58021 passes light engine through Doncaster station, heading for the nearby Doncaster Carr depot. The class could always be found in the Doncaster area, due to the large amounts of MGR coal traffic in the area. No. 58021 is currently stored at Alizay depot, northern France, and carries TSO livery.

No. 58021, 22 May 1994

No. 58021 is seen on passenger duty at Worcester during the open day in 1994. This was working top-and-tail along with No. 47186 on a rake of former Network South East Mk2 coaches. The loco carried Trainload Coal livery; it has had the logos removed, but retains the small diamonds near the cab door.

No. 58021, 7 February 1999

No. 58021 is seen stabled for the weekend at Grove Park EMU depot on the Southern Region with a rake of British Gypsum wagons. This depot is situated not far from Hither Green, which is appropriate as the loco carries *Hither Green Depot* nameplates.

No. 58021, 6 August 2000

No. 58021 is seen on display at Old Oak Common open day 2000. The loco carries Mainline blue livery, despite being in EWS ownership for four years. It also carries the name *Hither Green Depot*, and the plate includes an oast house.

No. 58022, 13 April 1985

No. 58022 rests at is home depot of Toton, along with other members of the class. Toton have always had the Class 58 allocated, until a few were transferred to Eastleigh very late on in their careers.

No. 58022, 25 July 1985

No. 58022 spends time stabled at Saltley, carrying red-stripe Railfreight livery. This loco would spend many years in storage at Crewe Diesel depot, and then Crewe Electric depot. This loco has been brought by the Ivatt Diesel Recreation Society, with the aim of using the frames to recreate LMS loco No. 10000.

No. 58022, 18 March 1990

No. 58022 stands at Toton depot while still carrying shabby red-stripe Railfreight livery. At the time, this livery was being replaced by Trainload Coal livery.

No. 58022, 17 May 1991

No. 58022 passes through Olton station on the Birmingham–Leamington Spa line with a loaded MGR working, bound for Didcot power station. The loco now carries Trainload Coal livery.

No. 58023, 16 March 1985

No. 58023 stands at Saltley depot, Birmingham, between duties. This loco had only been in traffic for one month, and is seen along with classmate No. 58002. No. 58023 would later be named *Peterborough Depot*.

No. 58023, 12 February 1991

No. 58023 passes Washwood Heath with an empty MGR working from Didcot power station. The loco carries Trainload Coal livery, and also carries a large Toton depot plaque on the secondman's cab side. The positioning of these plaques varied, with some on the cab side and some on the engine-room doors.

No. 58023, 7 March 1999

No. 58023 *Peterborough Depot* is seen at Saltley, wearing very dirty Mainline blue livery. This loco only had four months' service left, being stored in July 1999. It would spend the next seventeen years in storage; it was recently sold to Ron Hull Junior for scrap, but has since moved onto the Battlefield Railway, Shackerstone, for further storage.

No. 58024, 13 April 1985

No. 58024 rests at Toton depot under a threatening sky. Despite its work-stained appearance, No. 58024 had only been in traffic for two months, and is seen along with other classmates and also No. 20073.

No. 58024, 26 June 1993

No. 58024 runs light engine through Doncaster station, heading for Doncaster Carr depot. The loco carries Trainload Coal livery, and also has a Toton depot plaque on the cab side.

No. 58024, 29 July 1999

No. 58024 departs Washwood Heath with a rake of open wagons. No. 58024 carries EW&S maroon livery – one of just a handful to do so. This was another livery that sat well on this class, and this view shows the menial tasks that the class had to deal with towards the end of their careers.

No. 58024, 11 September 2000

No. 58024 passes Washwood Heath with an MGR working. At this time, withdrawals had started to be made to the class but, despite this, No. 58024 would see another two years' service, not being withdrawn until 2002. Upon withdrawal, this loco was sent to Spain for high-speed construction workings. It currently carries Continental Rail blue livery and the number L42, and has been sold to Transfesa.

No. 58025, 6 May 1985

No. 58025 resides at Saltley depot when only two months old. Despite the short age of the loco, the running number is already peeling off the loco. This would be another class member to be sent to Spain for high-speed construction workings; however, it was not sold to Transfesa. Instead it still belongs to DB Cargo, but is stored at Albacete depot, Barcelona, carrying the number L41.

No. 58025, 23 October 1991

No. 58025 lifts its loaded MGR working away from a signal check at Washwood Heath while heading for Didcot power station. The loco carries Trainload Coal livery.

No. 58026, 13 April 1985

No. 58026 is seen stabled at its home depot of Toton. This loco had only been in traffic for less than a week and, not surprisingly, is still in pristine condition. No. 58027 was also present on this day, in the same condition.

No. 58026, 22 April 1987

No. 58026 runs light engine through Nuneaton station, having possibly come from Daw Mill Colliery, which is situated just down the line towards Birmingham. The loco still carries red-stripe Railfreight livery.

No. 58026, 27 July 1992

No. 58026 runs light engine past Washwood Heath carrying Trainload Coal livery. The loco is seen in a very work-stained appearance; with their body shape, they must have been difficult to keep clean.

No. 58026, 22 July 1993

No. 58026 is seen one year on from the previous photograph, having been cleaned up. The loco is seen passing through Derby with an MGR working, which includes hoppers fitted with canopies to eliminate coal dust. No. 58026 would be another class member to be hired to Axiom Rail in France, and is currently stored at Alizay, carrying TSO livery.

No. 58027, 13 April 1985

No. 58027 is seen stabled at Toton depot, having only been accepted to traffic during that week. Hard to imagine at the time, but it would only have a serviceable career of fourteen years before being withdrawn in 1999.

No. 58027, 13 April 1985

No. 58027 is seen at Toton on the same day as the previous photograph, having been shunted round to the other side of the shed. No. 58027 would eventually find use in Spain on high-speed-line construction trains, and carries the number L52. It would be one of the three locos in Spain not to be sold to Transfesa; instead it still belongs to DB Cargo, and is stored at Albacete depot, Barcelona.

No. 58027, 5 July 1996

No. 58027 arrives at Acton light engine. Acton yard is an important yard in West London, being a holding point for some of the numerous aggregate workings in the area. No. 58027 carries Trainload Coal livery, but has had the logos replaced with Mainline logos.

No. 58028, 7 May 1985

No. 58028 rests at Saltley depot when less than a month old. The loco is seen surrounded by classmates, and would be another member of the class to only have a career of fourteen years, being withdrawn in 1999.

No. 58028, 24 July 1985

No. 58028 eases a rake of Continental vans through Doncaster station. Doncaster was always a great place to visit due to the large amounts of freight traffic, and there were always locos coming and going, with the works in the background. It would have been hard to imagine, but it was less than four years since the last of the Deltics passed through Doncaster in service.

No. 58028, 11 April 1990

No. 58028 passes through Derby station with an MGR working. By this time the loco had been repainted into Trainload Coal livery, and of note is the position of the Toton depot plaque on the cab door.

No. 58028, 5 September 1993

No. 58028 is seen on display at the Worksop open day of 1993. The loco is seen under one of the impressive semaphore signal posts, ready to depart the next day with an MGR working. Of note is the fact that it now rides on a set of bogies fitted to No. 58036 onwards from new, with the sandboxes on the outside. This proves that the bogies were swapped regularly between different class members.

No. 58029, 4 May 1985

No. 58029 rests at Saltley depot, having only been in service for three weeks. The red-stripe Railfreight livery certainly brightened up a loco scene that was dominated by BR blue at the time.

No. 58029, 27 January 1988

No. 58029 passes Washwood Heath light engine while heading for the nearby Saltley depot. All the buildings in the background have since been demolished and replaced with a dual carriageway.

No. 58029, 1 July 1996

No. 58029 eases through Derby station with an MGR working, which includes canopy-fitted wagons. The loco carries Trainload Coal livery, but with the logos replaced by Mainline logos. No. 58029 would be another class member sent to Spain for high-speed-line construction workings, being numbered L44. It would later be sold to Transfesa, along with another eight locos, based in Alicante.

No. 58030, 13 June 1998

No. 58030 stands at Wolverhampton station while on railtour duty. This Pathfinder railtour visited various places within the West Midlands, starting off with Redditch. There was a pair of Class 73s on the rear. No. 58030 carries EWS maroon livery. This loco would head off the Spain for high-speed-line construction trains, being numbered L46. It was later sold to Transfesa.

No. 58031, 2 November 1985

No. 58031 is seen stabled at Saltley depot, carrying red-stripe Railfreight livery, along with Nos 58012, 58033 and No. 20104, which also carries red-stripe Railfreight livery.

No. 58031, 1 July 1996

No. 58031 passes through Derby with an MGR working. No. 58031 carries Trainload Coal livery, but with Mainline logos. No. 58031 would be sent to Spain for high-speed-line construction work, and was later sold to Transfesa, carrying the number L45. Of note is that, while in Spain, it was named *Caballero Ferroviario*.

No. 58032, 22 October 1985

No. 58032 is seen at Lawley Street container terminal, having run round its MGR working. The loco has been in traffic for less than three months, and still looks pristine.

No. 58032, 24 February 1987

No. 58032 is seen passing through Peterborough with a Fletton fly-ash working. This was a regular working for the class in the 1980s, and used former two-axle cement Presflo wagons.

No. 58032, 19 March 1987

No. 58032 runs light engine towards Water Orton while carrying red-stripe Railfreight livery. No. 58032 would later be named *Thoresby Colliery*, and would be another loco to find its way to France. It is currently is storage at Alizay, northern France, carrying ETF livery.

No. 58032, 8 December 1990

No. 58032 departs from a signal check at Washwood Heath with a rake of loaded MGR wagons, heading for Didcot power station. The loco has not long been repainted into Trainload Coal livery.

No. 58033, 19 October 1985

No. 58033 is seen at Saltley depot on the day it was released to traffic. British Rail were hoping to build some of these locos for export, but no orders were received, and only the fifty were built.

No. 58033, 10 November 1991

No. 58033 is seen stabled at Saltley depot, having gained Trainload Coal livery. This loco would later go on to be repainted into EWS maroon, being one of just a handful to be treated.

No. 58033, 17 August 1995

No. 58033 runs through one of the centre roads at Doncaster station with an MGR working. The loco still carries Trainload Coal livery, but the black diamonds have been replaced with Mainline logos.

No. 58033, 8 February 2014

No. 58033 stands in long-term storage at Alizay depot, Rouen, northern France. The loco was hired to Axiom Rail, and carries TSO yellow livery; it was used on high-speed-line construction workings. Like the other twenty-two Class 58s in store at Alizay, there is little hope of No. 58033 returning to use.

No. 58034, 18 January 1986

No. 58034 *Bassetlaw* rests at Saltley, along with other members of the class. No. 58034 was only three months old at the time, and had only been named a month previously. Of note is the fact that No. 58034 carries a builder's plate underneath the running number, whereas No. 58005 alongside doesn't – also note how the Railfreight logo on the secondman's cab side has had to be repositioned to accommodate the nameplate. This is another Class 58 stored at Alizay, where it carries TSO livery.

No. 58035, 17 May 1986

No. 58035 is seen stabled at Saltley depot, along with other members of the class. This was the last Class 58 to be built with the earlier-style bogies, with the sandboxes not on view. Again, this is stored at Alizay, northern France, and carries TSO livery.

No. 58035, 5 September 1996

No. 58035 runs into the yard at Acton along with No. 60042. No. 58035 carries Trainload Coal livery, but with the logos replaced with Mainline logos. Of note is the replacement set of bogies received from a higher-numbered classmate.

No. 58035, 8 February 2014

No. 58035 is seen in long-term storage at Alizay depot, carrying TSO livery. It's sad to see all these locos in long-term storage, as they have plenty of work life left in them. There are twenty-three Class 58s in store at this location.

No. 58036, 1 March 1986

No. 58036 is seen on Saltley depot, Birmingham, when only two weeks old. This loco was the first class member fitted with the different-style bogies, with the sandboxes visible. This loco was selected to go on hire to Axiom Rail, and would eventually become another loco to be stored at Alizay; it currently carries ETF yellow livery.

No. 58036, 17 August 1986

No. 58036 rests at Bescot when six months old. Despite the hard work this loco has done, it still looks reasonably presentable. This view also shows the terrible state of the yard at Bescot.

No. 58036, 28 July 1992

No. 58036 is seen passing Washwood Heath with a loaded MGR working to Didcot power station. By this time, the loco had received Trainload Coal livery but, as can be seen, a couple of the engine-room doors are in plain grey livery.

No. 58037, 1 January 1993

No. 58037 spends New Year's Day 1993 stabled at Saltley. The loco is at the head of four other Class 58 locos and, as can be seen from the frost on the ground, it was a bitterly cold day. As a result, the locos are kept ticking over to prevent them from not starting when they were required for service.

No. 58037, 11 May 2001

No. 58037 rests at Saltley depot, having been repainted into EWS maroon livery, being one of just a handful to do so. The loco has also been named *Worksop Depot*, after the depot in the Nottingham coalfields. No. 58037 would eventually be scrapped at Eastleigh depot by European Metal Recycling in December 2013.

No. 58038, 6 September 1986

No. 58038 is seen stabled outside the office block at Saltley depot when just six months old. This loco was selected to go on hire to Dutch operator ACTS, and was exported in 2005 for four years before returning to the UK in 2009. While in Holland, it was renumbered as 5814 and carried VOS Logistics livery.

No. 58038, 29 July 1999

No. 58038 passes Washwood Heath with a loaded cartic working from Longbridge. These workings conveyed brand-new Rover cars for export. No. 58038 by this time had received a coat of Mainline blue livery, and would go on to spend time in Holland. Upon its return would be sent abroad again, this time on hire to Axiom Rail in France. At present it is stored at Alizay depot, Rouen, northern France, carrying ETF livery.

No. 58039, 9 August 1986

No. 58039 is seen stabled at Saltley depot, carrying red-stripe Railfreight livery, when only five months old. It would be named *Rugeley Power Station* the following month and so would lose the Railfreight logo from the cabside.

No. 58039, 14 November 1986

No. 58039 rests at Saltley depot a couple of months after being named *Rugeley Power Station*. Of note is the cast Railfreight logo fitted onto the front of the loco. Today Saltley depot has been demolished, the Class 58 is in store at Alizay in France and Rugeley power station is scheduled for closure.

No. 58039, 20 May 1990

No. 58039 stands on display at Doncaster Works open day 1990. The loco has just been through the works for an overhaul, which included a repaint into Trainload Coal livery. This view shows the *Rugeley Power Station* nameplate, complete with CEGB 'e' logo.

No. 58039, 8 March 1992

No. 58039 *Rugeley Power Station* is seen resting at Saltley depot, Birmingham. By this time most, if not all, of the class carried Trainload Coal livery. No. 58039 would be selected to be hired to Dutch operator ACTS, and was exported to Holland in 2003, returning in 2009. It was then sent on hire to Axiom Rail for use on high-speed-line construction work in France, and is currently stored at Alizay, northern France, carrying ETF livery.

No. 58039, 14 June 1998

No. 58039 is seen carrying EWS maroon livery at Hither Green depot, London. Towards the end of their careers, some of the Class 58s could be found working at unusual locations due to the Class 66s taking over many of the coal workings. By this time, No. 58039 had lost its *Rugeley Power Station* nameplates.

No. 58040, 29 March 1986

No. 58040 is seen at Saltley depot when less than a fortnight old. Due to the number of coal workings through the Birmingham area, most of the class visited Saltley when new. No. 58040 would later be named *Cottam Power Station*.

No. 58040, 11 July 1991

No. 58040 is seen working through Washwood Heath with an empty MGR working from Didcot power station. By this time, the loco had been repainted into Trainload Coal livery, and had been named *Cottam Power Station*. This was another member of the class to work for Axiom Rail, and can be found at Alizay depot, carrying TSO livery.

No. 58041, 18 April 1986

No. 58041 passes Saltley depot with a loaded MGR working. The loco is passing a Class 47 on a similar working; this just shows how busy the coal traffic used to be in the Midlands. No. 58041 was only three weeks old at the time, but it is already showing signs of being worked hard.

No. 58041, 9 February 1992

No. 58041 *Ratcliffe Power Station* is seen stabled at Saltley depot. By this time, the loco had been repainted into Trainload Coal livery. Of note is the extra panel on top of the handrails, especially when compared to No. 58007, which is stabled adjacent.

No. 58041, 11 April 1993

No. 58041 is seen stabled at Knottingley depot carrying Trainload Coal livery and the name *Ratcliffe Power Station*. In this view, the loco is starting to show signs of the hard work undertaken by this class of locos. Knottingley depot has always been a large out-base for coal-sector engines for the vast amounts of traffic associated with the nearby Drax power station.

Nos 58041 and 33202, 14 June 1998

No. 58041 is seen stabled at Hither Green depot, London, alongside No. 33202. At this point the loco still carries the name *Ratcliffe Power Station*. It would later be selected for export to Spain, and would be sold to Transfesa. It currently works out of Alicante on ballast workings, carrying the number L36.

No. 58042, 16 August 1986

No. 58042 is seen at Bescot holding sidings when less than two months old. The loco is surrounded by many older locos, including Class 20s, 31s, 45s and 86s.

No. 58042, 6 September 1986

No. 58042 rests at Saltley depot before it was named *Ironbridge Power Station*. It would receive the name three weeks later at the power station. It would carry the nameplate for ten years before the plate was removed; it would then receive the name *Petrolea*.

No. 58042, 9 March 1991

No. 58042 passes Washwood Heath with an empty MGR working from Didcot power station. The loco carries the name *Ironbridge Power Station*. This loco would go on to be hired to Axiom Rail, and is currently stored at Alizay depot, northern France, carrying ETF livery.

No. 58043, 5 April 1987

No. 58043 rests outside the office block at Saltley depot. The loco carries red-stripe Railfreight livery, and had been in traffic for less than twelve months.

No. 58043, 24 February 1991

Four years on from the previous photograph and No. 58043 can be seen again stabled outside Saltley depot. By this time, the loco had been repainted into Trainload Coal livery.

No. 58043, 5 September 1996

No. 58043 is seen departing Acton yard with a rake of two-axle aggregate hoppers. The loco carries Trainload Coal livery, but has had the coal diamonds replaced with Mainline logos. By this time, the loco had lost its Toton depot plaque from the secondman's cabside, and also the BR double arrow from the driver's cabside.

No. 58043, 9 April 2002

No. 58043 passes Washwood Heath with a rake of continuous welded rail wagons. This loco had just four months left in service, being withdrawn in August. It would then be chosen to be sent to work in Spain for GIF, along with sister loco No. 58041. They were later sold to Transfesa, and No. 58043 can be found working out of Alicante on high-speed-line construction workings, carrying the number L37. Of note is the fact that it has lost its second-series bogies in exchange for a set of older-style bogies.

No. 58044, 27 September 1986

No. 58044 stands at Saltley when only two weeks old. Despite the young age of this loco, it is already starting to look scruffy on the cab roof. The loco would go on to be named *Oxcroft Opencast*.

No. 58044, 20 February 1991

No. 58044 passes Washwood Heath with a loaded MGR working, heading for Didcot power station. This would be named the following year as *Oxcroft Opencast*. No. 58044 would be selected to be exported to Holland, working for Dutch operator ACTS. It would leave the UK in 2003, returning in 2009. It would then go on to be exported again, this time working for Axiom Rail, France. Unlike the other members of the class that were exported, No. 58044 is currently stored at Woippy Yard, near Metz, carrying ETF livery.

No. 58044, 3 August 1992

No. 58044 *Oxcroft Opencast* is seen passing Washwood Heath light engine. This view clearly shows the nameplate and crest. The loco carries Trainload Coal livery, and looks very respectable. No. 58044 later saw service in Holland working for ACTS and, upon its return, it was sent to France to work for Axiom Rail. It can currently be found stored in Woippy Yard, Metz.

No. 58044, 10 September 1995

No. 58044 is seen stabled at Saltley depot, Birmingham. The loco still retains its *Oxcroft Opencast* nameplates, but has had its Trainload Coal decals replaced with Mainline branding. All fifty of the class passed to Mainline when the freight sectors were introduced. No. 58044 would be stored in 1999, before being sent to Holland to work for ACTS.

No. 58045, 15 October 1986

No. 58045 stands on Saltley depot, having only been in service for a fortnight. At this time, Saltley was a major depot, being centrally placed, and serviced both freight and passenger locos.

No. 58045, 5 July 1987

No. 58045 is seen stabled at Saltley in the summer sunshine, along with classmate No. 58026. Both locos still retain red-stripe Railfreight livery, but would both later be repainted into Trainload Coal livery.

No. 58045, 1 July 1996

No. 58045 approaches Derby station with an MGR working. The wagons in the consist have been fitted with canopies to help prevent coal dust escaping. No. 58045 has been repainted into Trainload Coal livery but, by this time, the coal diamonds have been replaced with Mainline logos. The loco also still retains the Toton depot plaque – power station cooling towers – on the secondman's cabside.

No. 58045, 15 March 2001

No. 58045 is seen stabled on Saltley depot. This view shows the neglect that the Class 58s suffered towards the end of their careers, with No. 58045 carrying Trainload Coal livery, but with Mainline branding applied. The wagons in the foreground were on the depot for scrapping and were cut up where they stood.

No. 58045, 30 April 2001

No. 58045 stands at Rugby in rapidly deteriorating external condition. This view shows some of the menial duties the class had to work during their rundown, with No. 58045 at the head of a rake of sleeper wagons. At this time Rugby was about to be transformed, and it would be completely rebuilt, including some new platforms.

No. 58045, 11 May 2001

No. 58045 is seen at Lowestoft while on railtour duty. This was the Pathfinders Freightliner Phoenix Railtour, which originated at Crewe. No. 58045 worked the Ely–Lowestoft leg and, as can be seen, it had been spruced up for the event. While working The Bone Breaker Railtour in August 2002, No. 58045 struck the buffers at Walton-on-Naize at slow speed, which resulted in its condemnation. The loco was later purchased by the Class 58 Locomotive Group to act as a source of spares in the restoration of No. 58016, and the carcass of No. 58045 was finally scrapped by European Metal Recycling, at Kingsbury in October 2010.

No. 58046, 17 March 1997

No. 58046 is seen passing Milford Junction with an MGR working. There used to be vast numbers of MGR workings around the Yorkshire area, but today their numbers have dwindled. No. 58046 carries Mainline blue livery, and also carries the name *Asfordby Mine*. The loco had previously been named *Thoresby Colliery*.

No. 58046, 21 September 1999

No. 58046 is seen working through Southampton Central with a rake of loaded cartic wagons carrying Ford Transits. No. 58046 carries the name *Asfordby Mine*, and also carries Mainline blue livery. No. 58046 would later find employment in France, working for Axiom Rail on high-speed construction trains. It is currently stored at Alizay depot, northern France, where it carries TSO livery; there is little hope of it returning to traffic.

No. 58047, 29 July 1987

No. 58047 rests at Saltley depot, carrying red-stripe Railfreight livery. No. 58047 would go on to be named *Manton Colliery* in 1992. No. 58047 would be selected to be sent to Spain for high-speed construction trains, and was later sold to Transfesa. It can be found working in Alicante in Spain, carrying the number L51. As with the other Spanish-based locos, there is little hope of them ever coming back to the UK.

No. 58047, 1 September 1991

No. 58047 is seen on display at the Worksop open day, 1991. The loco is seen opposite the main event and, at this time, still retains red-stripe Railfreight livery. This was one of the last Class 58s to retain this livery. No. 58047 can currently be found working in Spain for Transfesa.

No. 58048, 29 January 1988

No. 58048 is seen at Saltley, carrying red-stripe Railfreight livery. The loco has just come off the fuel roads and will stable up to await its next turn of duty. No. 58048 lead an uneventful life before finally being named *Coventry Colliery*. The loco was stored in 2000 and has never turned a wheel since. The loco has recently found a home at the Battlefield line and is being returned to serviceable condition.

No. 58048, 26 July 1992

No. 58048 *Coventry Colliery* is seen passing Washwood Heath with a loaded MGR working, heading for Didcot power station. By this time, the loco had been repainted into Trainload Coal livery, while the nameplate also carries a British Coal logo in the top left-hand corner. No. 58048 was later painted into EWS maroon and is now at the Battlefield line, Shackerstone, being returned to serviceable condition.

No. 58049, 9 April 1991

No. 58049 is seen passing Washwood Heath with a loaded MGR working, heading for Didcot power station. The loco carries red-stripe Railfreight livery, and also the name *Littleton Colliery*. Like No. 58048, the nameplate of No. 58049 also carried a British Coal logo in the corner but, by this time, it had been removed following the sale of British Coal. Of note is that, despite being named, the loco doesn't carry a cast Railfreight logo on the cab front like other members of the class did.

Nos 58049 and 58022, 27 July 1992

No. 58049 *Littleton Colliery* is seen passing Washwood Heath, working in tandem with classmate No. 58022. Despite being fitted with multiple-working equipment, the class rarely worked in multiple; I would guess that this is a loco failure and rescue, rather than a genuine double-headed working. Both locos carry Trainload Coal livery, and are heading for Didcot power station.

No. 58049, 8 February 2014

No. 58049 is seen in long-term storage at Alizay depot, Rouen, northern France. The loco carries the ETF livery of yellow and black solebar, whereas No. 58004 to the right carries TSO livery, which is again yellow, but with a blue solebar. There are twenty-three members of the class stored at Alizay, and have been for many years, with little prospect of returning to service.

No. 58050, 10 August 1993

No. 58050 is seen stabled at Saltley depot, carrying Trainload Coal livery. This was the last member of the class to be built, and subsequently the last loco to be built at Doncaster Works. No. 58050 carries the name *Toton Traction Depot*, and was originally built with SEPEX wheelslip equipment. This was later removed before it entered service, but was incorporated into the Class 60 build.

No. 58050, 27 August 1995

No. 58050 is seen on display at Crewe Basford Hall open day, 1995. The loco had just been outshopped in Mainline blue livery; the repaint also included painting the *Toton Traction Depot* nameplate background into light blue. Being the last Class 58 built, this loco always seemed a popular choice to attend open days.

No. 58050, 30 August 1998

No. 58050 is again seen on open-day duty, this time at Toton in 1998. The loco had just been repainted into EWS maroon livery. Of note is the fact that the *Toton Traction Depot* nameplate has changed cabs and now sits underneath the driver's window, rather than on the secondman's cabside.

No. 58050, 10 April 2000

No. 58050 *Toton Traction Depot* is seen departing Washwood Heath's sleeper factory with a rake of brand-new sleepers. This traffic has operated for many years, and motive power has ranged from Class 31s through to modern-day Class 66s; it still runs today, with the new sleepers normally heading for Bescot, and then onwards to where they are needed.

No. 58050, 6 August 2000

No. 58050 *Toton Traction Depot* is seen on display at Old Oak Common open day, 2000. No. 58050 would later be selected to work in Spain on high-speed construction traffic. This is one of three that were never sold to Transfesa, and is currently stored at Albacete. As the last loco built at Doncaster Works, No. 58050 was selected to become part of the National Collection at York, but time will tell if it is returned to the UK to take its place.

No. 58048, 23 August 2016

No. 58048 is seen at the Battlefield Line, Shackerstone, having been preserved. The loco carries former EWS maroon livery but has had some replacement engine room doors fitted.